Little Pebble™
T0081109
All Kinds of Weather
Hot Weather
by Sally Lee
PEBBLE
a capstone imprint

Little Pebble is published by Pebble
1710 Roe Crest Drive, North Mankato,
Minnesota 56003
www.capstonepub.com

Copyright © 2019 by Pebble, a Capstone imprint. All rights reserved. No part of this publication may be reproduced in whole or in part, or stored in a retrieval system, or transmitted in any form or by any means, electronic, mechanical, photocopying, recording, or otherwise, without written permission of the publisher.

Library of Congress Cataloging-in-Publication Data
Names: Lee, Sally, 1943– author.
Title: Hot weather : a 4D book / by Sally Lee.
Description: North Mankato, Minnesota : Capstone, [2018] | Series: Little pebble. All kinds of weather | Audience: Ages 4-8.
Identifiers: LCCN 2018018348 (print) |
LCCN 2018019908 (ebook) | ISBN 9781977102027 (eBook PDF) |
ISBN 9781977101891 (hardcover) | ISBN 9781977101969 (pbk.)
Subjects: LCSH: Heat waves (Meteorology)—Juvenile literature. | Earth temperature—Juvenile literature. | Weather—Juvenile literature. | Summer—Juvenile literature.
Classification: LCC QC981.8.A5 (ebook) |
LCC QC981.8.A5 L44 2018 (print) |DDC 551.5/253—dc23
LC record available at https://lccn.loc.gov/2018018348

Editorial Credits
Marissa Kirkman, editor; Bobbie Nuytten, designer; Tracy Cummins, media researcher; Kris Wilfahrt, production specialist

Photo Credits
iStockphoto: skynesher, 5; Shutterstock: Daxiao Productions, 19, ER_09, 13, gpointstudio, 9, happystock, 15, Igor Vkv, Design Element, Nepster, 11, Studio 1One, 21, Thaweewong Vichaiururoj, 17, Tom Wang, 1, TXiXinXing, 7, V. Shvd, Cover, wowomnom, 12.

Printed in the United States 5594

Table of Contents

Whew 4

Why Is It Hot? 6

How Is the Weather? 12

Have Fun! 20

Glossary 22
Read More 23
Internet Sites 23
Critical Thinking Questions . . 24
Index 24

Whew

I play in the sun.

My skin is damp.

It is hot today!

Why Is It Hot?

The sun heats the earth.

Long days get more sunlight.

They are hotter.

Spring and summer
have long days.
They are warm seasons.

The earth tilts toward the sun in summer.

The sun's rays are strong.

They send more heat.

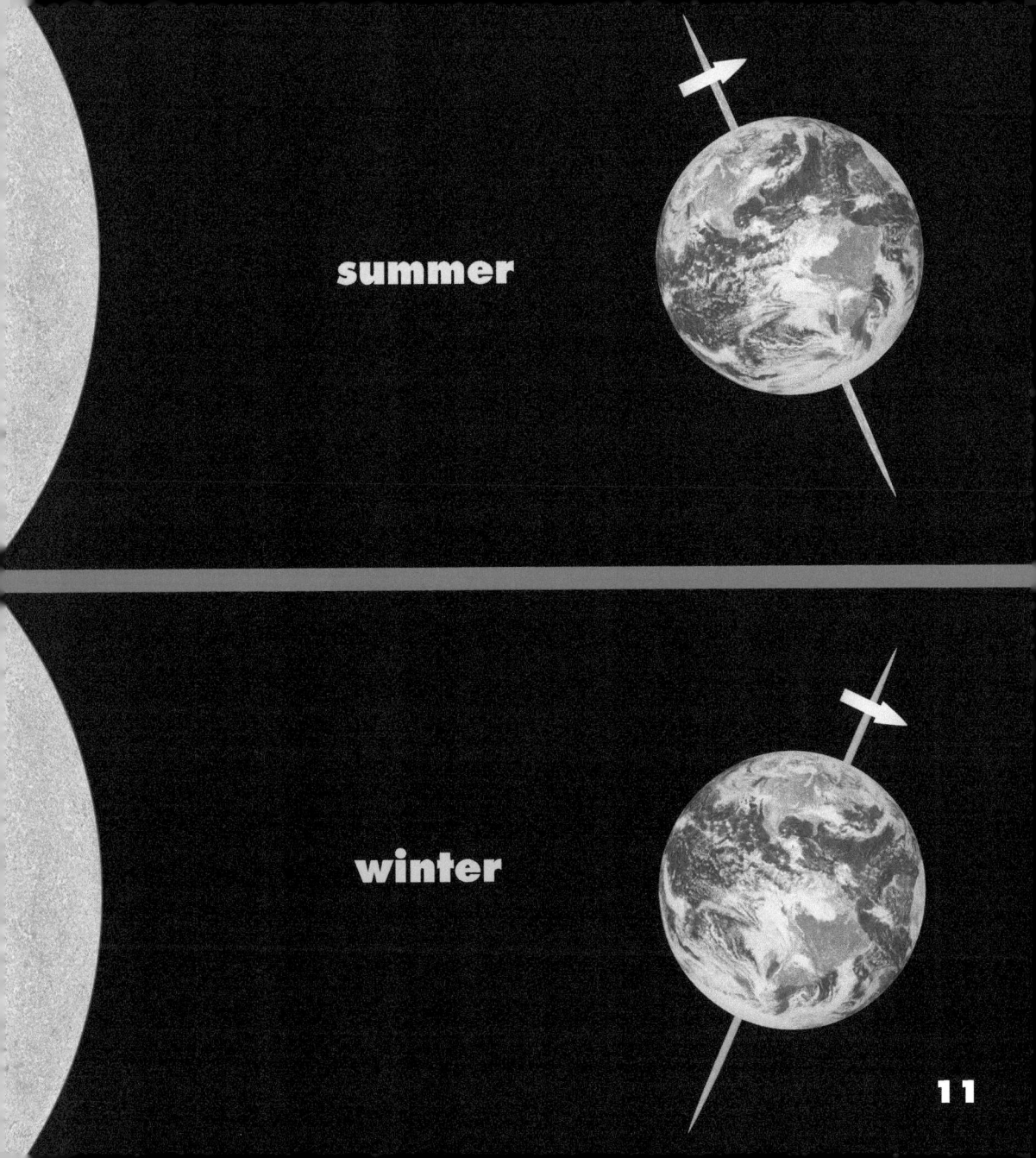
summer
winter

How Is the Weather?

Will today be cloudy

or sunny?

A forecast will tell you.

Clouds hide the sun.

The air feels cooler.

Clear days have more sun.

They feel hotter.

Humid days have moisture
in the air.
Your body's sweat
does not dry as fast.
You feel hotter.

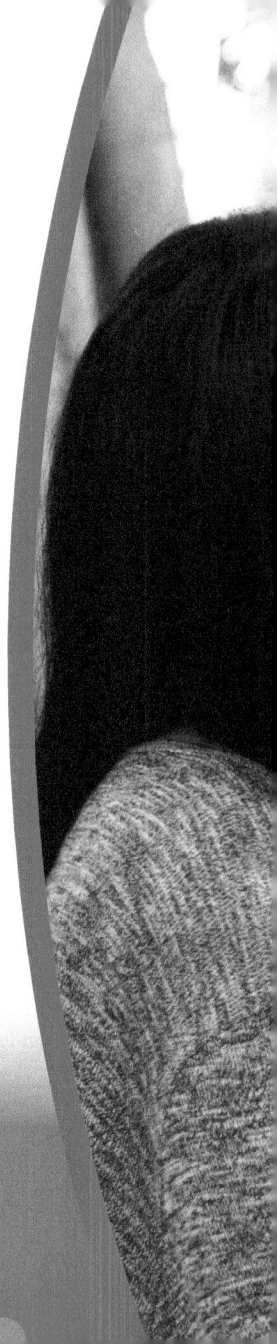

Whew!

The temperature is high

on a hot day.

Go inside if it gets too hot.

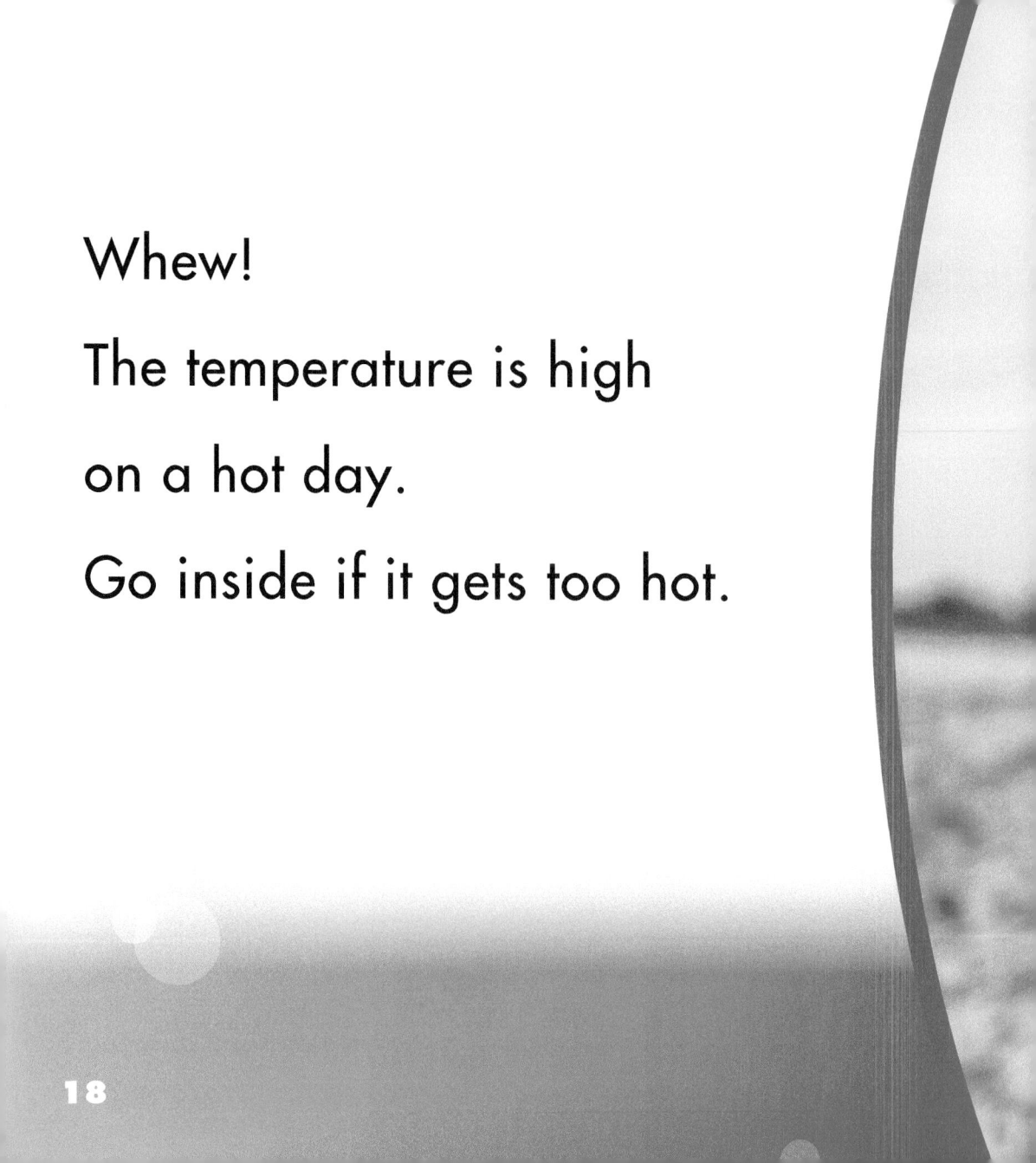

Have Fun!

Hot days can be fun.

Let's play in the pool.

Splash!

Glossary

forecast—a report of future weather conditions

humid—damp or moist

moisture—wetness

ray—a line of light that beams out from something bright

season—one of the four parts of the year; winter, spring, summer, and fall are seasons

sweat—to have salty drops of moisture come out through the pores in your skin

temperature—the measure of how hot or cold something is

tilt—an angle or lean; not straight

Read More

DeWitt, Lynda. *What Will the Weather Be?* Let's-Read-and-Find-Out Science 2. New York: HarperCollins, 2015.

Felix, Rebecca. *What Do People Do in Summer?* Let's Look at Summer. Ann Arbor, Mich.: Cherry Lake Publishing, 2014.

Rustad, Martha E. H. *Today Is a Hot Day.* What Is the Weather Today? North Mankato, Minn.: Capstone Press, 2017.

Internet Sites

Use FactHound to find Internet sites related to this book.

Visit www.facthound.com

Just type in 9781977101891 and go.

Check out projects, games and lots more at **www.capstonekids.com**

Critical Thinking Questions

1. Why are longer days warmer?
2. Why does the air feel cooler on a cloudy day?
3. What happens to your body on a hot day?

Index

air, 14, 16
clouds, 14
earth, 10
forecasts, 12
spring, 8
summer, 8, 10
sun, 4, 6, 10, 12, 14
sunlight, 6
sweat, 16
temperature, 18